EDINBURGH'S TRAMS, The La
Volume 2 – The South

by
R. J. S. Wiseman BA

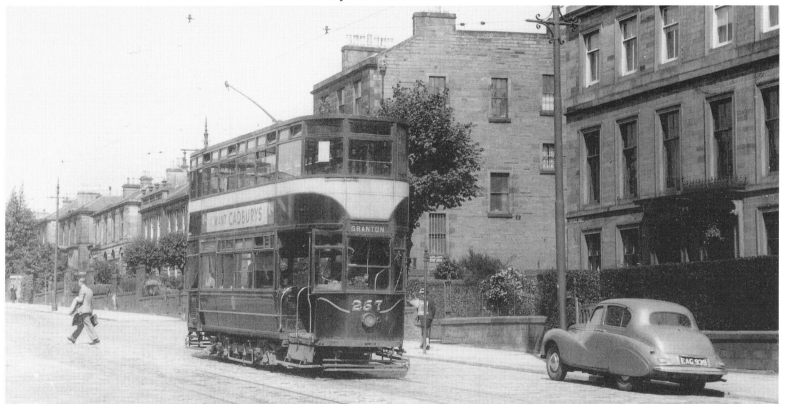

Three services, 3, 8 and 17, terminated at Newington Station. No. 257 (1932–55) is seen at Mayfield Gardens, just short of the station, where it will reverse. Today this residential district has many hotels and guest houses serving the increasing number of visitors to the city. *1 August 1953.*

© R. J. S. Wiseman 2005
First published in the United Kingdom, 2005,
by Stenlake Publishing Ltd.
Telephone: 01290 551122
Printed by Cordfall Ltd., Glasgow, G21 2QA

ISBN 1 84033 355 3

ACKNOWLEDGEMENTS

I would like to thank all those who have assisted with the production of this book, especially John Meredith who printed many of the photographs and George Fairley for his help in checking text and captions. I would also like to thank those who have provided additional photographs as credited.

FURTHER READING

The books listed below were used by the author during his research. None of them are available from Stenlake Publishing. Those interested in finding out more are advised to contact their local bookshop or reference library.

Brotchie, A. W., *Edinburgh, The Tramway Years*, N.B. Traction, 1979

Brotchie, A. W., *The Twilight Years of the Edinburgh Tram*, Adam Gordon, 2001

Hunter, D. L. G., *Edinburgh's Transport*, Advertiser Press, 1964

Hunter, D. L. G., *Edinburgh's Transport, The Corporation Years*, Adam Gordon, 1999

Stevenson, J. L., *The Last Trams*, Moorfoot Publishing, 1986

FOLLOW THE TRAM ROUTES ON LOTHIAN BUSES			
Tram service number and route	Tram abandonment date	Bus service number and destination	Notes
1, Fairmilehead	27 March 1954	7, Ferniehill; 37, 37A, Penicuik	Initially service 31. Extended to Hyvot's Bank
3, Newington Station	28 March 1953	3, Mayfield	
5, Morningside Station	30 October 1954	5, Oxgangs	
6, Marchmont Circle	26 May 1956	24, Royal Infirmary	West End, Tollcross, to Grange Road at Lauder Road only
7, Liberton	10 March 1956	7, Ferniehill; 37, 37A, Penicuik	
8, Newington Station	2 April 1955	8, Royal Infirmary	
11, 16, Fairmilehead	11 September 1956	11, Fairmilehead	
13, Churchhill via Tollcross	16 June 1956		No direct replacement. 5 covers Churchhill to Salisbury junction
14, Churchhill via Salisbury	16 June 1956		
15, Fairmilehead	18 September 1954	15, 15A, Penicuik	
17, Newington Station	10 March 1953		No direct replacement
19, Tollcross	26 May 1956		
23, Morningside Station	16 November 1956	11, Fairmilehead	
28, Braids	16 November 1956	11, Fairmilehead	

EDINBURGH'S TRAMWAYS – A BRIEF OVERVIEW

The first tramway in the City of Edinburgh was opened by the Edinburgh Street Tramways Co. on 6 November 1871 and ran from Haymarket via Princes Street and Leith Walk to Bernard Street in Leith. The company later extended its lines in Edinburgh and also in Leith and Portobello. On 9 December 1893 those lines in Edinburgh passed to the Corporation and were leased to Dick Kerr & Co. Ltd., which formed the Edinburgh & District Tramways Co. in 1894 to run the system. Three years later, in 1897, the company took over the cable lines to Goldenacre and Comely Bank which had been opened by the Edinburgh Northern Tramways Co. in 1888 and 1890 respectively.

The older routes had been horse-hauled, and with the exception of the line to Craiglockhart, were converted to cable traction in 1899–1901. The last horse tram ran on 24 August 1907 when Craiglockhart was converted to cable operation. The Edinburgh & District Tramways Co. also opened an electric tramway, to Slateford, on 8 June 1910. Leith Corporation took over the horse tramways in their area on 23 October 1904 and converted these to electric traction between 18 August and 21 November 1905.

On 1 July 1919 the City & Royal Burgh of Edinburgh Transport Department took over the cable tramways and the electric line to Slateford. The Burgh of Leith was amalgamated with Edinburgh on 20 November 1920, at which point the Leith electric tramways came under the control of Edinburgh. Work then started on phasing out the cable system, and electric traction was introduced between Pilrig and Liberton on 20 June 1922. The last cable tram ran on 23 June 1923. In the meantime the ex-Edinburgh Northern cable tramways to Goldenacre and Comely Bank were variously replaced by buses.

Electric traction was introduced from Hanover Street to Goldenacre on 8 June 1924 and to Comely Bank on 18 November 1923. The city also purchased the Joppa to Levenhall section of the Musselburgh & District Electric Light & Traction Co.'s line on 7 May 1931, which it had operated since 1 March. Many extensions were built, although the line to Crewe Toll was never completed and authorised extensions from Fairmilehead to Hillend Park, Liberton to Kaimes, and Stenhouse to Sighthill were never built.

THE SOUTHERN TRAMWAYS

This is the second book of four covering the tramways of Edinburgh as they existed between 1952 and their closure on 16 November 1956, the period in which most of the photographs were taken. This volume covers those routes which served the southern suburbs. These can be divided into four main groups. First those from Princes Street or Leith Street via North Bridge to Newington Station (services 3, 8 and 17) and Liberton (1 and 7). Second those routes via Princes Street, Lothian Road and Morningside to Braids (28) and Fairmilehead (11, 15 and 16). Third those linking the first two between Salisbury and Churchhill via Marchmont (5, 13 and 14) and also services 6 and 19 from Tollcross. Finally service 23 via the Mound to Morningside Station. Service 27 to Firrhill will be covered in the western volume.

By 1952 the tram fleet in Edinburgh could be divided into two main classes: old standard cars built between 1923 and 1934 and new standard cars dating from between 1933 and 1950. In addition there were eleven ex-Manchester cars bought in 1947 which do not feature in this book. All Edinburgh's trams were four-wheeled enclosed cars, the older ones having wooden bodies and the newer ones being either all-steel or of composite construction. The majority of the city's trams were built in the Shrubhill works. The exceptions were 71 older cars, of which 41 were built by Leeds Forge of Bristol; 20 by English Electric; and a further ten by Pickering of Wishaw.

The 118 new standard cars were derived from two experimental vehicles, Nos. 180 and 261, built at Shrubhill in 1932 and 1933 respectively. Of these, 34 all-steel cars were supplied during 1933–5: eleven by Hurst Nelson; fourteen by Metropolitan Cammell; and nine by English Electric.

A total of ten services, Nos. 1, 3 and 6 from Princes Street and Nos. 5, 7, 8, 13/14, 17 and 19 from Leith Street, turned on to North Bridge opposite Register House, crossing over the eastern side of Waverley Station. This picture shows the post office stop on North Bridge with Register House in the background. The island had two stops, the nearer one for services 7 and 17, plus services 1, 3 and 8 until their abandonment (on 27 March 1954, 28 March 1953 and 2 April 1955 respectively). Tram No. 145 (1935–56) is on service 6, the Marchmont Circle, and will wind its way back to the post office stop in 25 minutes by way of Salisbury and Tollcross. *11 April 1955.*

Continuing south over the bridges trams reached Nicolson Street, where this Saturday scene shows a pram parked outside Martin's shop, two buses on private hire and two motorcyclists heading towards the city. Tram No. 120 (1935–56) was operating service 5 to Morningside Station. *1 August 1953.*

Nicolson Street leads on to Clerk Street where No. 282 (1923–54), a Leeds Forge-built car, is seen on service 8 to Newington Station. A wide variety of shops and motor vehicles is in view. *1 August 1953.*

The junctions at Hope Park Terrace were reached a mile or so south of Register House. Service 19 turned into Hope Park Terrace here as it began its journey westwards, while until 25 March 1950 trams on service 18 from Princes Street via Tollcross to Liberton Dams, which travelled in the opposite direction, turned right out of Hope Park Terrace to continue their journey southwards. No. 167 (1935–55) is on service 5 and will continue along Clerk Street and Newington Road to the next junction at Salisbury Place, and there turn right for Grange Road as indicated by the board 'via Bridges and Grange Road' in the front windscreen. *1 August 1953.*

No. 18 (1935–56), a Hurst Nelson car, is turning into Hope Park Terrace from Clerk Street en route to Tollcross via Melville Drive. The following pages show the route to Liberton before returning to this location at Hope Park Terrace on page 14. *1 August 1953.*

Continuing south into Newington Road, a gradual incline preceded the next junction at Salisbury Place, with its post office and shops including Baird the Bootmaker, on the left. Beyond the junction is the dip down to Newington and the hills beyond. No. 251 (1932–56), on service 8, is heading north back towards the city. *3 July 1954.*

The same junction seen from Salisbury Place with No. 76 (1938–56) on service 5 turning into Newington Road en route to Piershill via Leith Street and London Road. Baird the Bootmaker's is again visible, along with Coopers grocery store. At the time of writing these premises were occupied by a cycle shop and an 'Early to Late' store. *27 May 1953.*

Looking back to the Salisbury Place junction from the south with No. 72 (1941–56) on service 8 heading for its terminus at Newington Station. Three trams are in sight in the background. Only services 3 (Stenhouse–Newington Station) and 18 had been abandoned by this time, so there was still plenty of tram traffic to be seen. The right-hand car could have been on service 1, 7 or 17, or might have been a 5 or 14 via Churchhill. On the left one tram is turning out of Salisbury Place, possibly on service 6, Marchmont Circle, while that in the background also heads for the city. *1 August 1953.*

Having continued south past Salisbury Place, No. 156 (1931–56) is travelling along Minto Street on service 8 to Newington Station down in the valley. The conductor has already anticipated the terminal crossover and has changed the destination screen to Granton. *25 May 1953.*

At one time Newington Station was the terminus of services 3, 8 and 17. Here the conductor of No. 59 (1947–56), on service 8, is turning the trolley in readiness for the return to Granton. The North British suburban railway serving the southern suburbs closed to passengers on 10 September 1962, but the line connecting Millerhill Yard via Niddrie to Haymarket is still used for freight. *1 August 1953.*

After the withdrawal of the 18, only two services, 1 and 7, continued south from Newington Station. Taken on an August Saturday, this animated scene at Lady Road shows cars, trams and a cyclist moving forward after passengers have alighted from No. 47 (1947–56) on service 1. It is closely followed by No. 214 (1940–56) on service 7. *1 August 1953.*

At Kirk Brae, Liberton Dams, trams on services 1 and 7 to Liberton reached the Braid Burn. The nurseries of the College of Agriculture are out of sight to the right, with Craigmillar Park golf course to the left. No. 235 (1936–56) was operating service 1. *1 August 1953.*

The steepest part of the climb up to Liberton is seen in this view of No. 26 (1935–56), built by Metropolitan Cammel, on service 7. The Daimler bus in the background is on service 18, which replaced the 18 tram on an extended route to Burdiehouse. *1 August 1953.*

No. 234 (1936–56) photographed at Orchard Head Road about halfway up Liberton Brae. *1 August 1953.*

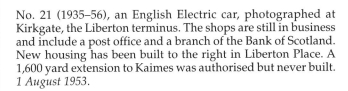

No. 21 (1935–56), an English Electric car, photographed at Kirkgate, the Liberton terminus. The shops are still in business and include a post office and a branch of the Bank of Scotland. New housing has been built to the right in Liberton Place. A 1,600 yard extension to Kaimes was authorised but never built. *1 August 1953.*

Hurst Nelson tram No. 18 (1935–56), on service 19 from Tollcross, turns north into Clerk Street at the Hope Park Terrace junctions on its journey via Leith Walk to King's Road, Portobello, to which it worked during the summer. The junction to the right (south) was used by service 18, Waverley – West End – Tollcross – Liberton Dams, until its abandonment on 25 March 1950. *1 August 1953.*

Hope Park Terrace leads into Melville Drive, a tree-lined avenue bordering The Meadows. No. 196 (1928–56) was photographed at the East Gate and is just about to cross into Hope Park Crescent on its way to the junction with Clerk Street. Beyond the trees on the right are tennis courts and bowling greens. *11 August 1953.*

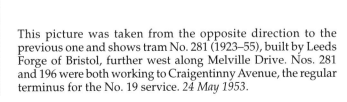

This picture was taken from the opposite direction to the previous one and shows tram No. 281 (1923–55), built by Leeds Forge of Bristol, further west along Melville Drive. Nos. 281 and 196 were both working to Craigentinny Avenue, the regular terminus for the No. 19 service. *24 May 1953.*

The sylvan setting of the junction with Marchmont Road is traffic-free in this photograph. No. 106 (1928–55) is heading to Tollcross, although the back screen has already been changed to Craigentinny Avenue in anticipation of the return trip. *23 May 1953.*

Having crossed The Meadows trams on service 19 entered Brougham Place by Leven Terrace before completing their journey at Tollcross by reversing on the crossover in Brougham Street. No. 19 (1935–56), an English Electric tram, has just left the terminus for Leith Walk and Craigentinny Avenue. *11 August 1953.*

Trams on the Marchmont Circle, service 6, ran in both directions to and from Waverley via Salisbury Place, Marchmont, Tollcross, Lothian Road and Princes Street. No. 56 (1935–56) is seen in Grange Road shortly after leaving the junctions in Salisbury Place. *25 May 1953*.

Looking east along Beaufort Road towards Grange Road from the junction with Marchmont Road as passengers board No. 204 (1935–56). St Catherine's Church, on the corner of Chalmers Crescent, dates from 1866. *26 April 1954.*

A 180° turn reveals No. 322 (1924–54) travelling in the opposite direction to No. 204 in the picture on the facing page and turning into Marchmont Road. Behind the tram is McGregor's of Marchmont, a grocers and provision merchants that celebrated its centenary in 2005 and is still run by the McGregor family. *4 April 1953.*

Marchmont Road, lined with fine houses, slopes gently down towards The Meadows, the trees of which can be seen in the background. No. 232 (1935–56) is about halfway along at Warrender Park Road on its way to the junction at Beaufort Road. *11 August 1953.*

Nearing the bottom of Marchmont Road and the junction with Melville Drive, the driver of No. 83 (1935–56) has obeyed the ALL DOWN CARS STOP HERE sign on the adjacent pole. The tram in Melville Drive is on service 19. *11 April 1955.*

Back on Melville Drive No. 69 (1934–56), the first of the new standard cars to be built at Shrubhill, has the road to itself as it speeds towards Tollcross. *11 August 1953.*

This final picture of Melville Drive shows No. 237 (1936–56) about to pass between a set of pillars as it enters Brougham Place. While they complement those at the east end of the drive (page 15), the two sets are not connected – those illustrated here formed the entrance to the International Exhibition of Industry, Art and Science of 1886. The tram will continue on the circular route via Tollcross and Lothian Road into Princes Street. *11 August 1953*.

Services 5 and 14 turned into or out of Salisbury Place from Newington Road, depending on which direction they were travelling in. In this view No. 76 (1938–56) is about to pass the junction with Causewayside (left) and enter Salisbury Place before turning left for the city centre. Beyond Causewayside is the Longmore Hospital, now closed. The tenement on the right has been demolished and replaced by a modern building for the National Library of Scotland. *25 May 1953.*

This photograph was taken at the western end of Strathearn Road, where there was a section of single line along Strathearn Place as far as Greenhill Place. Strathearn Place was a nineteenth century road built to bypass a narrow and circuitous route slightly to the south via Clinton Road and Kilgraston Road, which was used by the horse-drawn trams. The cable cars followed the new road to get to Marchmont. Tram No. 178 (1927–54), on service 13 to Granton, is seen at the crossroads with Whitehouse Loan about to leave the single line section. *4 April 1953.*

No. 366 (1929–55) was photographed further west along the single-line section in Strathearn Place. It is on service 5, heading for Morningside Station, even though the rear indicator shows Piershill. *4 April 1953.*

Back on double track, No. 254 (1932–56) is taking the corner into Greenhill Gardens. It is on service 14 to Granton via Churchhill (service 13 operated the same route anticlockwise via Salisbury Place). *4 April 1952.*

This picture shows Churchhill and the triangular junction with Morningside Road. Photographed from the south, No. 167 (1931–55), on service 5, is about to make the descent to its terminus at Morningside Station, although the driver's screen shows a mixture of Piershill and King's Road. *1 August 1953.*

The Churchhill services – 13 and 14 – used the tracks leading north (away from the camera). Here No. 357 (1929–55) is making for the city centre via Tollcross. Two of the churches that make up 'Holy Corner' are visible in the distance near the junction with Colinton Road. Nearest is the Baptist Church and beyond the Episcopal, while both the Parish Church (seen in the picture on the previous page), and beyond that the Congregational, are out of sight on the right. *11 August 1953.*

The northern terminus of services 23 and 27 was at Granton Road Station, and the two routes headed south through the city centre via Hanover Street, illustrated here. The driver of No. 37 (1949–56), on service 23, will cross Princes Street en route to the Mound with the help of the traffic policeman in the foreground. The front of an SMT bus and the back of an Alexander's Bluebird coach are also to be seen in the picture. *C. M. Wiseman, 18 April 1954.*

On the other side of Princes Street No. 116 (1930–55), also on service 23 but travelling in the opposite direction, has reached the bottom of the Mound and is passing the Royal Scottish Academy. On the left are Princes Street Gardens and in the background buildings with 1950s shopfronts which have since been replaced by glass and concrete structures. *19 April 1954.*

Against a background of the Old Town, No. 71 (1935–56) descends the Mound. Behind the tram is a floral crown commemorating the Queen's visit to Edinburgh following her coronation. The Writers' Museum of 1860 and Free Church of Scotland offices are to the left. Behind the tram is New College and the Assembly Hall, where the new Scottish Parliament debated for a time, and beyond that the tower of the Highland Tolbooth Church. *24 May 1953*.

Car No. 89 (1933–55) is seen crossing Chambers Street as it heads north along George IV Bridge, where it will continue over Lawnmarket to reach Princes Street by way of the Mound. This is an interesting part of the Old Town that has seen significant changes over the last 50 years. The buildings to the left of the tram have been demolished and replaced by an extension to the Royal Museum of Scotland, while the former church in the background is now the Bedlam Theatre. Out of sight to the left is the National Library of Scotland, while to the right and also out of sight is the (unchanged) Greyfriars Bobby pub and Greyfriars Church. *19 April 1954.*

The route of service 23 continued along Lauriston Place passing the Royal Infirmary (now closed) and George Heriot's School. This view looks back towards these two landmarks, which can be made out faintly in the background as Leeds Forge-built tram No. 310 (1923–54) approaches the descent to Tollcross. *19 April 1954.*

No. 60 (1929–55) has just left the Tollcross stop in Lauriston Place next to the labour exchange. At this time there was a desperate need to widen Earl Grey Street, which the tram has just exited. The building seen to the left of No. 60, plus everything to the right of the tracks in the pictures on pages 38 and 39, was subsequently demolished and the site lay vacant for many years until its recent redevelopment as a banking and commercial area. Removal of the old buildings allowed Earl Grey Street to be more than doubled in width. Modern flats now occupy the area to the right of the narrow and ancient roadway of High Riggs in the background. *11 August 1953.*

At the zenith of the tramway era there were seventeen services operating along Princes Street, giving access to all parts of the city. Here six trams are in view including No. 117 (1927–55), an extra working back to Tollcross depot, and No. 94 (1934–55), en route to Leith. *18 April 1954.*

Of the seventeen services serving Princes Street, ten turned left at the West End into Lothian Road. No. 39 (1938–56), on service 28 to Braids, was photographed adjacent to the Usher Hall (out of shot to the right). The tower of St John's Church at the corner of Princes Street is in the left background. *11 April 1955.*

Tollcross is a major intersection approximately half a mile to the south of the west end of Princes Street. Trams from four different directions once met here, making it equivalent in importance to the junctions at the Foot of Leith Walk. This picture was taken from West Tollcross looking down Earl Grey Street towards Lothian Road. The policeman has stepped aside to allow No. 212 (1940–56) to continue on its way to Shrubhill depot, its last journey of the day. The line to Tollcross depot is on the left, while the tracks to the right led to Brougham Street and the terminus of the No. 19 service. These lines were also used by Marchmont Circle cars on service 6. *11 August 1953.*

This photograph was taken on the same evening as the previous one and looks directly down Earl Grey Street. No. 269 (1935–56) is heading for Fairmilehead, while No. 76 (1938–56) is on service 15 to King's Road. The Central Hall, on the left, is the home of the Edinburgh Methodist Mission and the building behind tram 76 is Lothian House, now flats. *11 August 1953.*

In a third view taken on the same day, this time looking towards Earl Grey Street, No. 256 (1933–56) has just left the Tollcross loading island en route to Leith depot. The buildings on the right have since been demolished and replaced by modern premises. *11 August 1953.*

Looking down Home Street to Tollcross from the junction at Gilmore Place. No. 214 (1940–56) is on service 16 to Granton, while No. 280 (1923–54), a Leeds Forge-built car, is on service 23 to Granton Road Station. *11 August 1953.*

Trams encountered a slight gradient as they entered Bruntsfield Place approaching Bruntsfield Links (seen here on the left). No. 177 (1931–56) is on service 13 to Churchhill. *23 May 1953.*

Continuing south with the Barclay Church in the background and the trees of Bruntsfield Links to the right, No. 138 (1933–56), originally No. 29, is also on service 13. *11 August 1953*.

Bruntsfield terminus in Merchiston Place was not used by regular services. However, on weekday afternoons during term-time a tram came up from Tollcross depot at about 3.30 p.m., turned in this siding and ran as an extra via West End to Waverley. This was partly to relieve the pressure caused by the pupils of Boroughmuir and James Gillespie's Schools decanting at this time. Prototype tram No. 180 (1932–56) is seen here on an LRTA special tour, conveniently showing service number 23. This service originally terminated at Tollcross but was extended to the new siding in 1926, and then to Morningside Station on 28 July 1929. *31 July 1955.*

The next stop beyond Merchiston Place was at Colinton Road or 'Holy Corner' (see also page 28), with the Episcopal Church prominent in this photograph. Of the three trams in view in Morningside Road, No. 262 (1934–56) was one of three English Electric steel cars. It is on service 11 to Fairmilehead. *11 August 1953.*

The same tram photographed on the same service a week earlier descending from the Churchhill junctions. To the right is Morningside Church at Newbattle Terrace. The Bore Stone 'In which the Royal Standard was last pitched for the muster of the Scottish Army on the Boroughmuir before the Battle of Flodden 1513', was built into the wall of the church and is commemorated by the plaque seen here. *1 August 1953.*

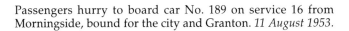

Passengers hurry to board car No. 189 on service 16 from Morningside, bound for the city and Granton. *11 August 1953.*

Looking north up Morningside Road from the corner of Canaan Lane (right) as two passengers board No. 149 (1931–55) on service 15. Fifty years ago traffic was light enough for motorists to overtake trams on what is now a very busy thoroughfare. *11 August 1953.*

When service 23 was extended to Morningside a siding was built in Belhaven Terrace, just to the south of Morningside Station (closed on 10 September 1962). Here No. 78 (1928–54, ex-No. 24) awaits departure time before returning to the city. *24 May 1953.*

Three services, 11, 15 and 16, ran to Braids and were later extended to Fairmilehead. An additional service, No. 28, was introduced in 1946 and terminated at Braids. Here No. 334 (1925–55), operating service 11, has Comiston Road almost to itself. Braidburn Valley Park lies to the left. *24 May 1953.*

Still on the Braid Hills but looking towards the terminus at Fairmilehead, No. 41 (1936–56), on service 15, waits by a shelter (still standing) next to an entrance to Braidburn Valley Park. *24 May 1953.*